Merry Christmas

2010

Smithsonian

Steps Out

Amy Pastan and Linda McKnight

Steps

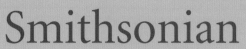

Smithsonian

Out

Collins
An Imprint of HarperCollinsPublishers

HarperCollins books may be purchased for educational, business, or sales promotional use. For information please write: Special Markets Department, HarperCollins Publishers, 10 East 53rd Street, New York, NY 10022.

FIRST EDITION

All images © Smithsonian Institution, except as noted.
The name of the "Smithsonian," "Smithsonian Institution," and the sunburst logo are registered trademarks of the Smithsonian Institution.

Designed by Linda McKnight, McKnight Design, LLC
Edited by Anita Schwartz
The authors would like to thank Ellen Nanney of Smithsonian Business Ventures for coordinating this project. Her efforts made this book series possible.

Library of Congress Cataloging-in-Publication Data
Pastan, Amy.
    Smithsonian steps out / Amy Pastan and Linda McKnight.
        p. cm.
    ISBN 978-0-06-125151-1
1. Shoes--History--Exhibitions. I. McKnight, Linda, 1947- II. Title.

TT678.5.P37 2007
391.4'13—dc22   2007018457

07 08 09 10 11   TP   10 9 8 7 6 5 4 3 2 1

The authors would like to thank the following Smithsonian museums, research centers, and offices for their assistance and cooperation in the making of Spotlight Smithsonian books:

Anacostia Community Museum
Archives of American Art
Arthur M. Sackler Gallery
Cooper-Hewitt, National Design Museum
Freer Gallery of Art
Hirshhorn Museum and Sculpture Garden
National Air and Space Museum
National Air and Space Museum's
    Steven F. Udvar-Hazy Center
National Anthropology Archives
National Museum of African Art
National Museum of American History,
    Kenneth E. Behring Center
National Museum of the American Indian
National Museum of Natural History
National Portrait Gallery
National Postal Museum
National Zoological Park
Smithsonian American Art Museum
    and its Renwick Gallery
Smithsonian Institution Libraries
Smithsonian Institution Archives
Smithsonian Astrophysical Observatory
Smithsonian Center for Folklife
    and Cultural Heritage
Smithsonian Environmental Research Center
Smithsonian Photographic Services
Smithsonian Tropical Research Institute
Smithsonian Women's Committee,
    Office of Development

Beaded Moccasins

Crow
Hide with glass beads
National Museum of the American Indian

Smithsonian Steps Out

The Smithsonian has been called "The Nation's Attic" because its collections are so eclectic and so vast. But it might just as easily be called "The Nation's Closet" for all the shoes, shoe accessories, and shoe imagery it holds. Where can you see all kinds of footwear from Dorothy's ruby slippers to Superman's boots, beaded moccasins to ceramic cowboy boots, a Tuareg anklet from Africa to a lunar overshoe from the Apollo space mission? From heels to high tops, fringed leggings to Olympic ice skates, Manolo Blahnik mules to Celia Cruz's sling backs—the Smithsonian has it all. Among the wealth of items in its collections are many treasures for those fascinated by footwear. But with seventeen museums and a zoo in Washington, D.C., two museums in New York City, various research centers, and more than 137 million objects in all, the Smithsonian can be overwhelming—even for those who have the opportunity to come often. *Smithsonian Steps Out* offers a selection of unique items from the collections and allows you to see them as no other visitor can. In these pages you can experience highlights from the exhibits as well as see lesser-known items that are seldom on view. Jump from Sonja Henie's ice skates at the National Museum of American History to shoe-shaped matchsafes at the Cooper-Hewitt, National Design Museum. Find a shoe drawing by Wayne Thiebaud at the Archives of American Art along with 1970s platform shoes from the Anacostia Community Museum. Enjoy the world's largest museum, cultural, and scientific complex without planning a trip, fighting the crowds, or wearing down the soles of your sneakers. And return as often as you like.

Group of Matchsafes

Late 19th century–early 20th century
Various makers
United States, Europe, England
Silver, lacquer, wood, and other materials
Cooper-Hewitt, National Design Museum
Gift of Stephen W. Brener and Carol B.
Brener

Matchsafes were manufactured in the late nineteenth and early twentieth centuries, not just to keep matches safe and dry, but to advertise products as well. For example, the Hood Rubber Company of Boston made a matchsafe of vulcanized rubber in the shape of a boot. Food and beverage companies produced matchsafes to resemble everything from biscuits and chocolate bars to champagne bottles. There is a wealth of shoe matchsafes in the collection of the Cooper-Hewitt, National Design Museum.

1965-66 Season Poster for the Municipal Theater, Basel, with Weekly Program (Saisonplakat Stadttheater, Basel mit Wochenspielplan)

1965
Designer: Armin Hoffmann
Offset lithograph on white wove paper
Cooper-Hewitt, National Design Museum
Gift of Ken Friedman

This poster from the 1965-1966 season of the Basel Municipal Theater cleverly juxtaposes photographic reproductions of several objects closely associated with theatrical, dance, and musical events. From left, we see a classical column, a boot with a spur, a ballet dancer's leg "en pointe," a music stand, and the lower part of a cello.

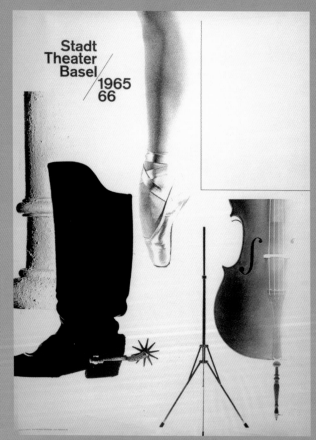

Ann Miller Posing with Her Shoes

1984
Jeffrey Ploskonka
Black and white photographic print
Smithsonian Institution Archives

Among the finest tap dancers in the history of the American musical, Ann Miller (1923-2004) appeared in many classic films, such as *Easter Parade* (1948), *On the Town* (1949), and *Kiss Me Kate* (1953). She wore these gold-painted, high-heeled dance shoes many times throughout her career, as well as to perform 500 taps per minute for *Ripley's Believe It or Not*. The shoes have "jingle taps," fitted in the heels, which produce greater sound. Miller is seen here donating the shoes—nicknamed "Joe" and "Moe"—to the Smithsonian in 1984.

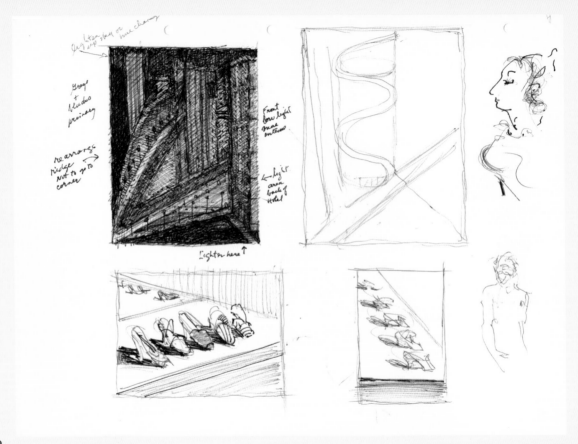

San Francisco Street Scene, Women's Shoes, Figure Studies

c. 1990
Wayne Thiebaud
Sketch
Archives of American Art
Wayne Thiebaud Papers
Art©Wayne Thiebaud/Licensed by VAGA,
New York, NY

American artist Wayne Thiebaud (b. 1920) is well-known for his paintings of cakes and pastries. Because he depicts items of mass culture, he is often associated with the pop art movement. This page from one of Thiebaud's sketchbooks is a delightful sample of the artist's style. It includes a shoe store window, a city scene, and figure studies with the artist's handwritten notations.

The Hunter

1980
Fernando Botero
Oil on canvas
Hirshhorn Museum and Sculpture Garden
Gift of the artist, 1980

Colombia-born Fernando Botero
(b. 1932) is a master of wit and
satire. By increasing the proportions
of his figures—often monstrously
exaggerating hands, feet, torso, and
props—he creates bizarre but funny
caricatures. This pudgy hunter carries
a huge firearm and strides forward
in giant boots. His dog's body has
ballooned to the point where his feet
hardly seem to support him. Botero
takes his subject matter from the
villages of his native country as well as
from Italian Renaissance and Spanish
Baroque paintings.

Flagg Bros

1975
Robert Cottingham
Oil on canvas
Hirshhorn Museum and Sculpture Garden
Museum purchase, 1976

During the 1970s, artist Richard
Cottingham (b. 1935) traveled across
the United States, taking photographs
of trains, cities, and signage. He
used those images as sources for his
paintings. Cottingham was particularly
fascinated with commercial signs—like
this bold one for Flagg Bros Men's
Shoes—not only because they have
artistic merit, but also because he found
that signs trigger memories. This image
does, in fact, have a nostalgic feel to it,
reminding many viewers, perhaps, of
the shoe store in the town where they
grew up.

Qualicraft Shoes/
Chinese Lady

1974
Richard Estes
Color silkscreen on paper mounted on
paper-clad aluminum
Hirshhorn Museum and Sculpture Garden
Museum purchase, 1977
© Richard Estes, Courtesy Marlborough
Gallery, New York

Looking very much like a real store
window, this color screenprint of
"Qualicraft Shoes" is actually a
landscape by photo-realist artist, Richard
Estes. Estes' prints have sharp details
and meticulously finished surfaces,
reminiscent of photography. Most of his
work documents street scenes in New
York. Some combine different views into
one composite scene. They are typically
devoid of people and convey a sense of
isolation.

The Skateboarders Project (36)

2000
Nikki Lee
C-print on Fujiflex mounted on plastic panel
Hirshhorn Museum and Sculpture Garden
Anonymous gift, 2004
© Nikki S. Lee, Courtesy Leslie Tonkonow
Artworks + Projects, NY

A participant in her own works of art, Nikki Lee (b. 1970) chooses a culture to document, and then changes her appearance, mannerisms, and behaviors to become one of its members. She takes snapshots of herself actively involved in the new community she has joined. Lee has "become" a yuppie, an older woman, an exotic dancer, and a teenage Latina. Here she puts on some serious hi-tops and "becomes" a teen skateboarder.

Tim Brauch Skateboard

c. 1998
National Museum of American History
Division of Music, Sports, and Entertainment
Gift of Frank, Joan, and Kristy Brauch

This Santa Cruz skateboard helped Tim Brauch (1974-1999) step out and win the 1998 Vans Triple Crown Championship. Skateboarding grew out of roller skating in California and was influenced by surfing. Brauch, known for his speed, agility, and devotion to skateboarding, was a true champion and raised the sport to a new level. He participated in the World Cup and other international events, displaying an independent spirit that earned him recognition and appreciation from the skating community. Brauch died suddenly of a heart attack at the age of twenty-five. There are Web sites, championships, and skateboard parks named in his honor.

The Golden Days

1944-1946
Balthus
Oil on canvas
Hirshhorn Museum and Sculpture Garden
Gift of the Joseph H. Hirshhorn Foundation,
1966
©Artists Rights Society (ARS), New York/
ADAGP, Paris

A dainty slippered toe protrudes
prominently in this suggestive canvas
by Balthus (1908-2001). It belongs
to an adolescent girl, who gazes
dreamily at her own reflection before
the golden light of the fire. While
the awkward teen years hardly seem
"golden," Balthus may be referring
to the emerging beauty of youthful
girls—many of whom spend those years
daydreaming, like this self-absorbed
subject.

Prosthetic Leg

n.d.
National Museum of American History
Division of Science and Medicine

During the Civil War, this type of
prosthetic was used to replace a severed
foot. Seven of ten wounds suffered
by soldiers in that conflict were to
extremities. Amputation was the most
common surgery performed. A surgeon
cut the anesthetized patient's skin and
muscle to expose the bone and then
severed the bone with a bone saw.
These saws earned physicians of the day
the nickname "sawbones."

Untitled

1990
Robert Gober
Wax, cotton, wood, leather, shoe, and
human hair
Hirshhorn Museum and Sculpture Garden
Joseph H. Hirshhorn Purchase Fund, 1990

This disembodied leg, complete with
shoe and sock, is the work of sculptor
Robert Gober (b. 1954) and is part
of the permanent collection of the
Hirshhorn Museum and Sculpture
Garden. In Gober's art, the ordinary
becomes strange and the mundane
takes on surreal proportions. Gober uses
simple objects to explore themes such
as childhood, home, religion, sexuality,
victimization, and transcendence.

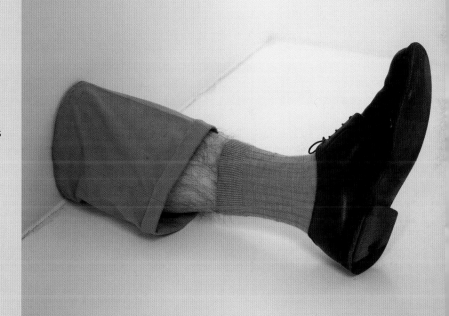

(Right) *Superman Boots*

c. 1954
National Museum of American History
Division of Music, Sports, and Entertainment
Gifts of D.C. Comics

Here are the boots that helped the man of steel "leap tall buildings at a single bound." Superman has delighted many generations of comic book readers, radio and TV enthusiasts, and film-goers. Today, Superman artifacts attract visitors of all ages to the Smithsonian's National Museum of American History. The boots at left were made for Christopher Reeve for his role as Superman in the 1987 film, *Superman IV: The Quest for Peace*. The pair on the right was created for George Reeves in the popular TV series, *The Adventures of Superman* (1952-1958). In addition to these boots, the museum has both Reeve's and Reeves' full costumes.

Combat Boots

Worn c. 1950-1952
National Museum of American History
Division of Military History and Diplomacy

These World War II-era leather combat boots have leather tops with cuffs fastened by buckles. Handwritten in ink on the inside of one cuff is "RUSSELL HATCH 57100176."

Beaded Sneakers

n.d.
Tom and Kathy Wegman
Smithsonian Women's Committee
Office of Development

Artists Tom and Kathy Wegman use brilliantly-colored beads to transform everyday items into objects of wonder. These elaborate sneakers with Native American motifs seem like a cross between an athletic shoe and a moccasin. Married since 1987, the couple's artistic partnership is very strong. They have shown their work together at the Smithsonian Craft Show, as well as in galleries throughout the United States.

Dorothy's Ruby Slippers

1939
From the movie *The Wizard of Oz*
National Museum of American History
Division of Music, Sports, and Entertainment
Anonymous donor

This pair of ruby slippers worn by Judy Garland (1922-1969) in the MGM film *The Wizard of Oz* in 1939 is one of the most popular artifacts in the Smithsonian. The appeal of these shoes crosses generations. Toddlers and their grandparents seem equally transfixed by the sparkling pumps that enabled Dorothy and her dog Toto to get home from Oz to Auntie Em's house in Kansas. The magical shoes were first created by L. Frank Baum in his 1900 novel. When adapting the novel for film, MGM Studio changed the color from silver to red. Several pairs of ruby slippers, created by chief costume designer Gilbert Adrian, were used throughout the shooting of the movie. This pair was used in dance scenes.

Cowboy Boots

1980
William Wilhelmi
Slip-cast, airbrushed-underglaze and glazed
porcelain with gold lusters
Smithsonian American Art Museum
Gift of the artist

These appear to be the ideal pair of
cowboy boots—until you venture to
put your feet inside. Made of clay, they
are from the Smithsonian American
Art Museum and are a visual joke on a
symbol of the American West. Painted
with a starry and cloudy sky above a
desert dotted with cacti, the boots are
exquisite in color and detail. The artist,
William Wilhelmi (b. 1939), may know
a great deal about cowboy boots from
having lived in Texas.

High-topped Fringed Leggings

Cowhide, glass beads
National Museum of the American Indian

This elaborate footwear was created
by Indians of the southern Plains who
combined moccasins with leggings to
create high-topped boots. Worn by
women, they are a fashion statement,
with intricately designed and sewn
beads running down the sides. Boots
such as these are made of supple
hides. In earlier times, preparing the
hides for footwear and other clothing
was a woman's task. A woman
skillful at processing such hides
earned considerable prestige for her
accomplishments.

Group of Young Men Making Boots

1880
John N. Choate
Glass negative
National Anthropological Archives

The boot shop at the Carlisle Indian Industrial School in Pennsylvania was photographed by John Choate in 1880. The school was the first off-reservation boarding school for Native American children. Founded by Richard Henry Pratt, its mission was to assimilate Native American children into white American culture—to "civilize" them. To achieve this, Pratt ordered young Indians to abandon their customs, languages, and religions. Pratt's so-called "noble experiment" failed miserably, but not before taking both an emotional and physical toll on the thousands who passed through Carlisle's gates.

Woman's Leather and Fabric Shoe from the Carlisle Indian School

1880-1890
National Museum of American History
Division of Home and Community Life,
Costume Collection

This shoe was made at the Carlisle Indian Industrial School in Carlisle, Pennsylvania. There, the boys and girls were forbidden to wear native dress, speak native languages, and practice native customs. It is not known what happened to the young child who may have made this shoe, but many of the children at Carlisle were overworked and mistreated, and hundreds died of disease. The school closed in 1918.

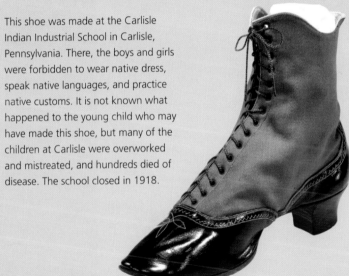

White Mountain Apache Moccasins

Deerhide uppers, cowhide soles, glass beads, and sinew
National Museum of the American Indian

These Apache moccasins have crosses on them—signifying the faith of the owner and the importance of the shoes in Apache culture. They may have been used in religious ceremonies or dances, as well as in everyday life. Women generally sewed the beadwork on Apache footwear. The distinctive round toe of the moccasins protected the foot from rocks, cactus, snakes, and other dangers.

Moccasins

19th and 20th centuries
National Museum of the American Indian

Moccasins by many native cultures are seen in this photograph, illustrating the diversity of style and artistry among native tribes. Moccasins were the perfect shoes for early natives because they protected feet from the elements, but were also flexible and conformed to the land. In the frigid climate of the north, they were made of sealskin and often came up to the knee. In the warmer deserts of the Southwest and Mexico, a lighter sandal was worn.

Anklet

Mid-late 20th century
Tuareg Peoples
Macina region, Mali
Metal
National Museum of African Art
Gift of Jerome Vogel

The Tuareg peoples live in West and North Africa. A Tuareg woman probably wore this elaborately decorated anklet for festivals and on holidays. Tuareg women often inherit jewelry from their mothers or receive it as gifts from their husbands when they marry. Silver is associated with clarity and happiness, so this object would have been highly valued. It is one of the many unique examples of silver work in the Smithsonian's National Museum of African Art.

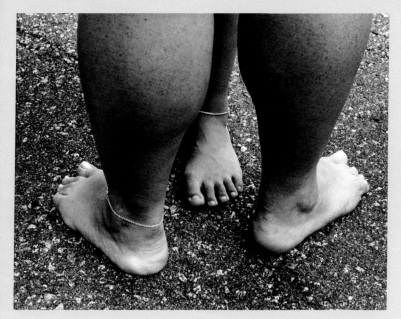

Three Feet

Date unknown
Bernard Stadiem
Silver print
Smithsonian American Art Museum
Gift of the artist

Bernard Stadiem (1930-2005) created this intimate portrait of three feet. The larger pair may belong to a mother, and the small foot between them, to her child. Each of them wears an ankle bracelet, suggesting that these two people are closely linked. The photograph has a sculptural quality, and the gritty ground adds an interesting texture to the print.

Collection J. Benyoumoff - Rep. int.

Dakar—Fils d'un Chef

[Son of a Wolof Chief, Dakar, Senegal]
c. 1912
Hand-colored postcard, collotype
Published by J. Benyoumoff
Eliot Elisofon Photographic Archives
National Museum of African Art

The orange shoes are not the only items that draw the viewer to this photograph of a dignified gentleman in the Senegalese harbor town of Dakar. Notice the cane, vase of flowers, and backdrop of an interior courtyard. Early in the twentieth century, African patrons chose to pose for such photographs because they wanted to project a modern and sophisticated lifestyle. The effect was greatly enhanced by a colorist, who expertly added the lush golds, reds, pinks, and purples to the photograph, which was printed as a postcard.

"The Torn Christmas Stocking"

c. 1882-1883
Advertisement for Samuel M. Lederer's
"Popular Downtown Store," New York
Warshaw Collection of Business Americana
Archives Center, National Museum of
American History

Filled to overflowing, this stocking may have torn from holding so many holiday trinkets. The image, from around 1882-1883, may have been used in an ad for Mr. Lederer's "Popular Downtown Store" in New York. Presumably, Lederer offered a wealth of goods, something for everyone's Christmas stocking. The original item may be seen in the Christmas Section of the Warshaw Collection of Business Americana, at the Archives Center, National Museum of American History.

Ida McKinley Boots

1897
Beaded satin
National Museum of American History,
Division of Politics and Reform

Ida McKinley was beautiful and well educated, qualities that first drew William McKinley, who became America's twenty-fifth president, to her. She served as America's first lady from 1897-1901 and wore these elegant boots to the 1897 inaugural ball. Sadly, Ida suffered from depression and seizures during her time in the White House. Her husband remained devoted to her until he was assassinated in 1901.

We Both Must Fade (Mrs. Fithian)

1869
Lilly Martin Spencer
Oil on canvas
Smithsonian American Art Museum
Museum purchase

The lovely Mrs. Fithian is the subject of this portrait by artist Lilly Martin Spencer (1822-1902). Adorned with lace and pearls, and clothed in a dazzling blue gown, Mrs. Fithian looks out at the fading light of the window and holds a withered rose in her hand. She seems to be aware that, like the light and the rose, her beauty will fade. Her slippered foot, peeking out from beneath her gown, points directly at the viewer, reminding us, perhaps, that we too are not immune to time.

Scottish Pipes Band

Smithsonian Folklife Festival 2003
Color photograph
Smithsonian Center for Folklife and
Cultural Heritage

The 2003 Smithsonian Folklife Festival
featured more than one hundred of
Scotland's finest musicians, storytellers,
craftspeople, cooks, and scholars. They
came to Washington, D.C., to share
aspects of Scottish culture. The City
of Washington Pipe Band turned out
for the opening ceremonies. Wearing
traditional kilts, knee socks, and boots,
the pipe and drum players welcomed
Scottish visitors, dignitaries, and
participants to the National Mall.

Latina Dancer in Front of Smithsonian Castle

Smithsonian Folklife Festival 2004
Color photograph
Smithsonian Center for Folklife and
Cultural Heritage

In the summer of 2004, the National
Mall was pulsating with the rhythms
of "Nuestra Música," a program
sponsored by the Smithsonian Folklife
Festival. Presenting the Latino face of
American life through music and dance,
it featured mariachi bands and Latina
dancers wearing glamorous costumes.
Visitors might have noticed the
glittering heels of the dance troupe.

First Pressure Suit

1934
Developed by Wiley Post with B. F. Goodrich
National Air and Space Museum

Wiley Post (1898-1935) was the first
pilot to fly solo around the world. His
aircraft, the *Winnie Mae*, is on view at
the National Air and Space Museum's
Udvar-Hazy Center. The Museum also
owns the first practical pressure suit,
which he helped develop in 1934. The
body of the suit has three layers: long
underwear, an inner black rubber air
pressure bladder, and an outer suit
made of rubberized parachute fabric.
This was complemented by pigskin
gloves, leather boots, and an aluminium
diver's-style helmet. The suit was first
used in flight on September 5, 1934,
during which Post reached an altitude
of 40,000 feet above Chicago.

Woman Inspecting Lunar Overshoes

c. 1968
International Latex Corporation
Gelatin silver print photograph
National Air and Space Museum Archives

The National Air and Space Museum has many intriguing photographs in its archives. This image, taken during the Apollo lunar missions, shows a woman inspecting lunar overshoes with Mylar and Kapton insulation, which would be worn on missions to the moon. While they look like props from a science fiction movie, such insulated footwear protected the astronauts from low temperatures in space and allowed them freedom of movement.

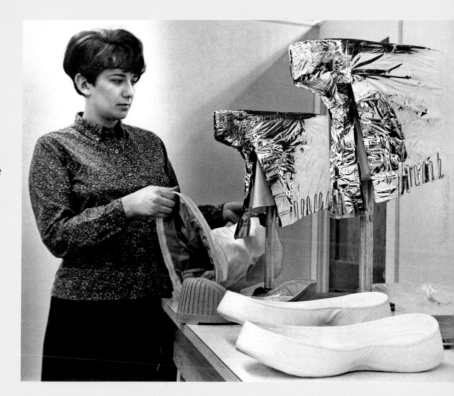

Skylab Personal Artifacts

1970s
National Air and Space Museum

Skylab was the first space station that the United States launched into orbit. It stayed in space from 1973-1979 and was visited by crews three times in 1973 and 1974. Some personal artifacts from Skylab are in the collection of the National Air and Space Museum. Among them are foot restraint shoes fitted with triangular metal cleats, designed to fit into the Skylab decking. NASA also gave the Museum some of the astronauts' tools, clothing and personal hygiene items, and spare packages of food.

Boot from Apollo Space Suit of Dr. Harrison Hagan Schmitt

1972
Apollo 17 Lunar Mission
National Air and Space Museum

The crew of *Apollo 17*—Mission commander Captain Eugene A. Cernan, command module pilot Commander Ronald Evans and lunar module pilot Dr. Harrison Schmitt—flew the last manned lunar mission of the Apollo era in December 1972. During the *Apollo 17* mission, Cernan and Schmitt landed their lunar module *Challenger* at Taurus-Littrow on the edge of the Sea of Serenity. For the next three days, they spent more than twenty-two hours working on the Moon, during which Schmitt wore these cumbersome-looking but effective shoes.

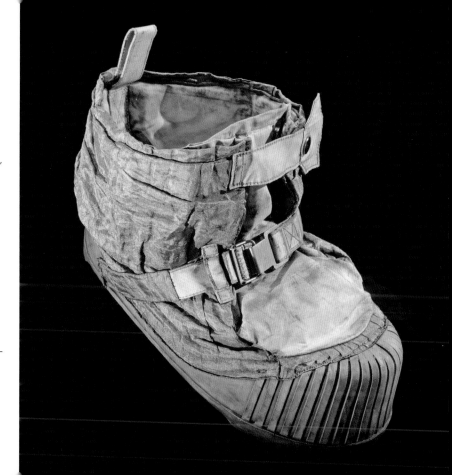

The Shoe Carriage.

The Nest fight.

Shelter.

Bait for the birds &c.

The Ogre considering whether Com. will go down.

The Commodore conquers his rival.

Com. riding his own Hobby.

The Com. out generals the Ogre and escapes with his Boot.

The Com. has t 'on a string?

COMMODORE NUT, AS HOP O'MY THUMB,

IN THE PLAY OF

THE GIANT AND HIS SEVEN LEAGUE BOOTS.

Now performing at

Barnum's American Museum,

NEW-YORK.

Lith. & Pub. by N. Currier, N. York.

n.d.
Nathaniel Currier
Colored lithographic print
National Museum of American History
Harry T. Peters "America on Stone"
Collection

This colored print advertised the play *The Giant and His Seven League Boots*, presented at Barnum's American Museum. It shows scenes from the production in which Commodore Nutt plays the character Hop O'My Thumb. The little Commodore is quite the hero, vanquishing a rival many times his size and popping up in all kinds of interesting hiding places that are many times his size, including a shoe, spoon, bottle cap, and the giant's boot. The Peters Collection houses many fine lithographs by the firm of Currier & Ives, as well as other outstanding prints from the nineteenth century.

STEWARDESS IS YOUR:

SMILE, Friendly & Sincere
POSTURE, Erect & Poised
HAIR, Short & Styled
MAKE-UP, Neat & Natural
BLOUSE, Fresh & Pressed
RIBBON, New & Trimmed
NAILS, Manicured & Polished
GLOVES, White & Tailored
UNIFORM, Clean & Pressed
PURSE, Orderly & Polished
SHOES, Repaired & Shined

?

SMILE!

Frontier Airline Stewardess

c. 1953-1955
Unidentified photographer
Gelatin silver print photograph
National Air and Space Museum Archives

Are her shoes "repaired and shined"? A stewardess for Frontier Airlines performs a last-minute flight check on her uniform before reporting for duty. In the early days of airline travel, crews were a lot more formal in dress and demeanor. Air travel was a luxury limited to very few and customers were truly pampered. In those days, there was certain glamour in being a stewardess, right down to the shoes.

Five African American Girls Wearing Ballet Costumes and Shoes

c. 1948
Scurlock Studio Records, c. 1905-1994
Gelatin silver print
Archives Center , National Museum of
American History

The Scurlock Studio Records are held
in the Archives Center at the National
Museum of American History. The
collection documents African American
life in Washington, D.C. through most
of the twentieth century. These lovely
young ballerinas, dressed perhaps for a
performance, show off their toe shoes
and tutus in this group shot from the
late1940s. An unknown boy stands at
center.

Abigail Adams' Shoes

n.d.
Leather and embroidery
National Museum of American History,
Division of Politics and Reform

These fancy dress shoes belonged to Abigail
Adams (1744-1818), the second First Lady
of the United States and the first to live in
the newly constructed White House. Mrs.
Adams was highly intelligent, independent,
and keenly interested in politics. During the
American Revolution, she ran the family farm
in Braintree, Massachusetts, by herself, while
her husband labored for independence at the
Continental Congress in Philadelphia, and
traveled on diplomatic missions to France
and The Hague.

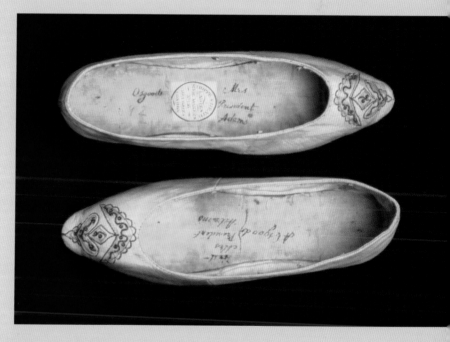

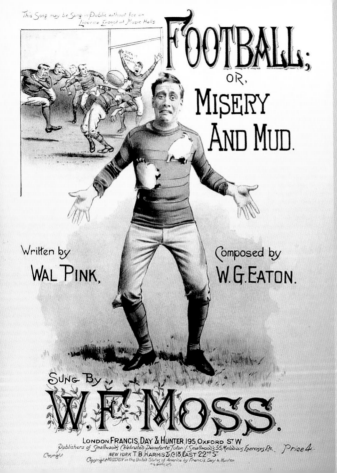

"Football; or Misery and Mud"

1894
Sheet music
Archives Center
National Museum of American History
Sam DeVincent Collection of Illustrated
American Sheet Music

At the turn of the twentieth century, football cleats were fairly low-tech, but the game was just as dirty as it is today. The cover of this sheet music shows an early football player who is a bit worse for wear. There are songs for practically every sport, and the Sam DeVincent Sheet Music Collection has a delightful selection of sports sheet music. Most of the lyrics relate to a particular university or club team, but "Misery and Mud" doesn't seem to have been composed with any particular institution in mind.

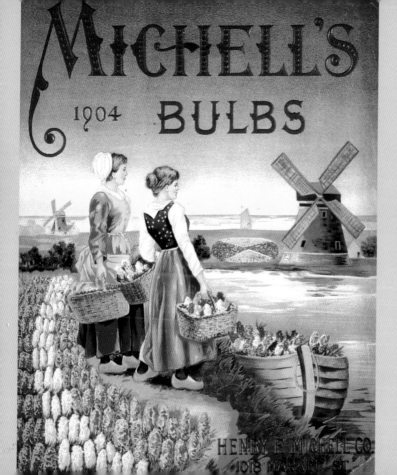

Michell's Bulbs

1904
Henry F. Michell Company
Philadelphia, Pennsylvania
Smithsonian Institution Libraries

This landscape is quintessentially Dutch, right down to the clogs adorning the feet of the young women. It graced the cover of *Michell's Bulbs*, one of about 10,000 seed and nursery catalogs dating from 1830 to the present in the Smithsonian Institution Libraries. Swiss immigrant Henry F. Michell started his retail seed business in an attic on Philadelphia's Market Street in 1890. His brother Frederick joined him in 1892, and in less than a decade the business prospered and expanded. Today the business has its headquarters in King of Prussia, Pennsylvania.

49

Woman's Shoes, "Orientalia" Mules

1986-1995
Designer: Manolo Blahnik
National Museum of American History
Division of Home and Community Life,
Costume Collection

Manolo Blahnik (b. 1943) grew up in the
Canary Islands off the coast of Spain.
After studying architecture and art in
Paris, he came to New York in 1971.
His portfolio was reviewed by *Vogue*
magazine editor Diana Vreeland, who
encouraged him to design shoes. Blahnik
first designed mules with beading over
the instep for Paloma Picasso in 1986.
He then later produced them in a variety
of fabrics, including this black and white
sample with metallic gold leopard spots,
beaded in semi-precious stones and
baroque pearls.

Silver Shoes Worn by Celia Cruz

n.d.
On loan to the National Museum
of American History
Courtesy of the Celia Cruz Foundation

Celia Cruz was a legendary singer
best known as the "Queen of Salsa."
She left her native Cuba in 1960 and
came to live in New York City in 1962.
She became part of the ever growing
and influential Latin music scene,
and the only woman to make it in
the male dominated world of salsa
music. Her flamboyant style made her
performances dynamic and memorable.
Most of her shoes were custom made
for her in Mexico by shoemaker Nieto.
The open-toed swan-heeled example is
decorated with rhinestones.

Wedding Shoes

1865
Salem, Massachusetts
White leather
National Museum of American History
Division of Home and Community Life,
Costume Collection

Ellen Jane Knight wore these lovely
white leather wedding shoes on
August 19, 1865, the day she married
Henry Bradford in Easthampton,
Massachusetts. They were made by a
shoemaker in Salem, Massachusetts.
Mrs. Bradford's descendants donated
them to the costume collection at
the Smithsonian National Museum of
American History.

Platform Shoes and Afro Pick

c. 1970s
Anacostia Community Museum
Gift of Pearline Waldrop

Cool platform shoes and large Afro picks were ubiquitous accessories among younger generation African Americans in the 1970s. This pick's handle is shaped into a fist, a sign of the Black Power Movement. It also has a peace sign, a symbol of the anti-war movement during the Vietnam conflict. Both items come from the Anacostia Community Museum's collection, which preserves artifacts of African American culture.

Ice Skates Signed by Sonja Henie

c. 1945
National Museum of American History
Division of Music, Sports, and Entertainment

Three-time Olympic gold-medalist Sonja Henie (1912-1969) brought glamour to ice-skating. Her athleticism and theatricality thrilled audiences. Her short skirts and white skates became the standard skating costume and her spectacular moves set the bar high for competitors. After winning medals in the 1928, 1932, and 1936 Olympic games, Henie signed a movie contract with Twentieth Century-Fox. Success of the film *One in a Million* (1936) made her one of Hollywood's leading actresses, but her greatest legacy, perhaps, was inspiring young girls to skate.

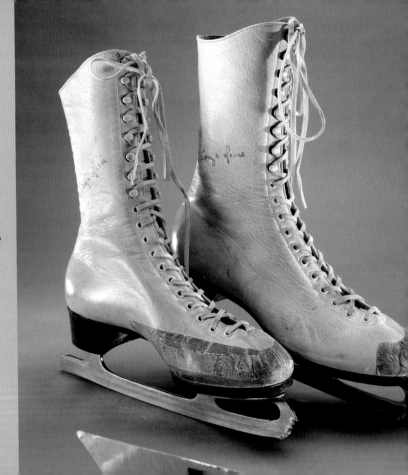

Brian Boitano's Skates

1988
National Museum of American History
Division of Music, Sports, and Entertainment

U.S. ice skating star Brian Boitano wore these Harlick skates in the 1988 Olympics at Calgary, where he battled Canada's skating champion Brian Orser for the gold—and won! The boot company added the American flags for good luck. The Boitano-Orser match captured world attention and was attended by record-breaking crowds. The "Battle of the Brians" has become Olympic legend.

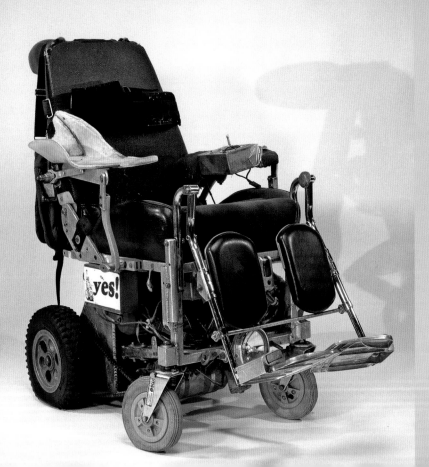

Ed Roberts' Wheelchair

c. 1978
National Museum of American History
Division of Medicine and Science

Ed Roberts was paralyzed by polio in 1953, when he was just fourteen years old, but that did not stop him from getting around. In the 1960s, while a student at the University of California at Berkeley, he pioneered a program for disabled students. Later, his efforts expanded into a worldwide campaign—called Independent Living movement—to obtain equal access and civil rights for those with disabilities. Roberts' wheelchair has a sports-car seat, go-cart wheels, and can achieve a top speed of eight miles per hour.

James L. Plimpton Skate Prototype

c. 1860
National Museum of American History
Division of Music, Sports, and Entertainment
Gift of Elizabeth Plimpton

James Plimpton (1828-1911) invented and patented a rollerskate that revolutionized the sport. Rather than have the wheels affixed directly to the plate of the skate, he had his wheels turn like those on a wagon—independent of the plate—so the skate could "rock" more easily when the skater simply leaned to one side. The Plimpton skate was a huge success and with Plimpton's support, the first roller rink was opened in 1866 in Newport, Rhode Island.

Pi tan e sha a du, Man & Chief, Principal Chief of the Pawnees

c. 1857
Nebraska
McClees Gallery, Julian Vannerson (agent and photographic artist)
Emulsion etched on glass negative
National Anthropological Archives

Dressed in impressive leggings, this chief was the first signer of the treaty of 1857 in which four Pawnee tribes ceded land to the U.S. government in return for protection. Pi tan e sha a du was openly accepting of white settlers and even accompanied a delegation of his tribe to Washington, D.C., on a diplomatic mission as early as 1825. He was a good orator and frequent speaker at Indian councils. Pi tan e sha a du died in 1874 from an accidental pistol shot.

Farrier's Box

Early 20th century
National Museum of American History
Division of Work and Industry
Gifts of Dr. and Mrs. Arthur H. Greenwood
and Theodore R. Hile, Jr.

This horseshoer's box was built from a simple packing crate, allowing it to be easily carried from hoof to hoof. The tools were rugged and accessible—once used they could be tossed back into the tray without breakage. A good, no-nonsense chest, this box has no frills or decoration, but probably well-served the farrier who owned it to outfit many hard-working horses with new shoes.

Swim Fin, Patent Model

1940
Vulcanized rubber
National Museum of American History
Division of Music, Sports, and Entertainment
Gift of Owen Churchill

Owen Churchill (1896-1985) patented the rubber swim fin and radically altered the sports of scuba diving and snorkeling. A gold medalist in the eight-meter yacht race at the 1932 Los Angeles Olympics, Churchill, ironically, was not a proficient swimmer. He had seen Tahitian swimmers attach woven leaves to their feet to propel them through water, which gave him the idea to make swim fins of rubber. Ridges on the sides allowed swimmers to move through water at a greater speed.

Carl Ben Eielson

n.d.
Unidentified photographer
Toned gelatin silver print
National Air and Space Museum Archives

This undated photo of explorer and aviator Carl Benjamin Eielson shows him warmly clothed and posed with snowshoes. Eielson learned to fly during World War I and after the war, joined an air club that did barnstorming stunts. He later moved to Alaska and flew the first air mail there. He is best known for flying the first airplane across the Arctic Ocean in 1926 and for his flight over the North Pole in 1928. Eielson also helped establish Alaskan Airways. He died in an air crash in 1929 while attempting to rescue passengers of a cargo vessel trapped in ice in the Bering Sea.

Shoe Roller Skates

n.d.
Thomas Wegman
Glass beads on skates
The Smithsonian Craft Show
Sponsored by the Women's Committee,
Office of Development

The Smithsonian Craft Show is one
of America's premier juried craft
exhibitions. Founded in 1983, it is
presented each year by the Smithsonian
Women's Committee and benefits
education and outreach programs at
the Smithsonian. This pair of unique
roller skates by Thomas Wegman is
an example of the craftsmanship that
may be seen at the show. Colorful,
humorous, hip, and expertly made,
these are the skates everyone wants,
but only one lucky buyer can own.

Untitled

1946
Gelatin silver print
Anacostia Community Museum
Lee Harris Papers
Gift of Mr. Harris Lee

These adorable siblings—Lee and
Renée Harris—pose on Easter morning
in New York City in 1946. Showing
off what appear to be brand new
clothes purchased for the holiday, Lee
doffs his hat at the photographer and
Renée strikes a pose that shows off
her fashionable suit and squeaky clean
white shoes.

Saidie Sellyna

c. 1919
Unidentified photographer
Gelatin silver print
Anacostia Community Museum Archives
Sullivan Family Collection
Gift of Savina and Dominga Martin and
Donna Akiba Sullivan-Harper

The woman in the bejeweled costume and provocative T-strap heels is Saidie Sellyna, an actress, singer, and dancer. Her image is in the Sullivan Family Collection at the Anacostia Community Museum. The collection consists of four generations of letters, artifacts, and photographs from an African American family that migrated to the United States from Nova Scotia in 1883.

911 Attacks on World Trade Center Artifacts: Mayor Giuliani's Boots

Worn 2001
National Museum of American History
Division of Military History and Diplomacy

Mayor Giuliani wore these boots when he visited the site of the World Trade Center in the days following the terrorist attacks of September 11, 2001. His leadership was key to the city's recovery.

911 Attacks on World Trade Center Artifacts: Maria Cecilia Benavente's Shoes

Worn 2001
National Museum of American History
Division of Military History and Diplomacy

Maria Benavente wore these black slip-ons as she evacuated her office on the 103rd floor of the South Tower of the World Trade Center. On hearing that the North Tower had been hit, Maria acted quickly, descending the stairs to the 78th floor and catching the express elevator to the ground. She carried her shoes to make exiting faster. Seventeen minutes later, the South Tower she had just vacated was hit, cutting off all escape paths for those who remained above the 78th floor.

Timmy's Sneakers

c. 1957
Keds Sneaker Company
National Museum of American History
Division of Music, Sports, and Entertainment
Gift of Jon Provost

What is childhood without sneakers? This pair of classic Keds hi-tops was worn by child actor Jon Provost (b. 1950), who played "Timmy" on the television series *Lassie* (1957-1964). These sturdy shoes allowed him to run and play with the famous collie in style and comfort. Provost even doodled on the rubber soles with a marker, just like any other kid. Sneakers were invented in the early 1900s and haven't gone out of style since.

Native American Hoop Dance

September 2002
Color photograph
National Museum of the American Indian

The inaugural ceremonies for the opening of the National Museum of the American Indian on the National Mall brought together tribes from all regions of the United States. Derrick Davis, a world champion hoop dancer, is seen performing at the inaugural powwow. His beautifully detailed costume is complemented by beaded and fringed boots.

Credits

Smithsonian image numbers are followed by names of the photographers, when known.

p.2 2000-110055
p.3 2004-50562 by Hugh Talman
p. 5 11.008 by David Heald
p. 7 photo by Matt Flynn
p. 8 1997-19-44
p. 9 84-15191-34
p. 10 AAA_thiewayn_0009
p. 12 80.111
p. 13 76.96
p. 15 77.25
p. 16 04.13
p. 17 2004-11286
p. 19 66.347
p. 20 2004-51195 by Eric Long
p. 21 90.15
p. 22 2004-50562 by Hugh Talman
p. 23 99-41050
p. 24 263325.000
p. 25 81-5294
p. 26 1981.107A-B
p. 27 T207749
p. 28 NAA Choate Glass Negative
06802900
p. 29 2000-4627
p. 30 16.7349 by David Heald

p. 31 photo by David Heald
p. 32 2002-23-6
p. 33 2003.14.2
p. 34 SG-20-12
p. 35 digital, NMAH
p. 36 2004-5714
p. 37 1970.101
p. 38 2003-42780 by Hugh Talman
p. 39 2004-34843 by Richard Strauss
p. 40 96-15179
p. 41 83-15833
p. 42 NASM-9A00353
p. 43 2004-39274
p. 44 2003-24658
p. 45 86-11868
p. 46 618n10050585
p. 47 92-2444
p. 48 digital
p. 49 digital
p. 50 2000-110055
p. 52 digital, NMAH
p. 53 digital
p. 54 digital, NMAH
p. 55 digital, Anacostia
p. 56 2004-11291

p. 57 2004-29840
p. 58 A-02-01-13
p. 59 2004-11287 by Eric Long
p. 60 BAE Glass Negative 02180a
p. 61 91-9498
p. 62 2004-11288
p. 63 83-21561
p. 65 digital
p. 66 2003.7078.053
p.67 2005.7002.005
p. 68 2006-12370
p.69 2002-3659
p. 70 digital, NMAH
p. 71 2002-15323 by James Di Loreto

Cover: *Beaded Sneaker*
n.d.
Tom and Kathy Wegman
Smithsonian Women's Committee
Office of Development

Silver Shoe Worn by Celia Cruz
n.d.
On loan to the National Museum of
American History
Courtesy of the Celia Cruz Foundation